Introduction

Our daily lives, it seems, have the capacity, on one hand, to get us all wound up, or on the other, to grind us down to nothing at all. In today's world, especially, instant communication, 24-hour "everything," and schedules overflowing with responsibilities, activities, and difficulties demand every last drop of attention we have. As a result, stress levels soar, energy levels plunge, and priorities become confused.

However, in the midst of it all, a still, small voice deep within whispers to our souls: "You are worried and distracted by many things; there is need of only one thing. Come to me, all you that are weary and are carrying heavy burdens, and I will give you rest" (Luke 10:41-42; Matthew 11:28). These words of Jesus are meant for you and me—for all who are anxious and weary.

Our Christian faith does not promise us tranquil, trouble-free lives, but it does offer us support and strength along the way as we focus on the "one thing necessary." Jesus came to save us, to build us up, and to help us live joyful and fruitful lives in God's service. He does this through the gifts provided us in prayer, Scripture, worship, the sacraments, and the tradition of the Church with all its members who form the Body of Christ. In other words, Jesus offers us *holy* rest, so that we may place our priorities in order, and then address them peacefully and attentively. With this sacred rhythm at the center of our being, we can live *in* the world without being *of* the world (cf. John 17:13-16; Romans 12:2).

The five chapters in this book—originally published by Abbey Press Publications as individual titles in the *Catholic Perspectives CareNotes* series—inspire us to look to Jesus in the Gospel tradition handed on to us through the Church. He is our peace (Ephesians 2:14). I pray this book helps you to rediscover and embrace this wonderful mystery—24 hours a day, seven days a week.

—Br. Francis Wagner, O.S.B.

pathways

When Anxious and Weary

Edited by Br. Francis Wagner, O.S.B.

Path of Life Publications
Spiritual Food for the Christian Journey from **Abbey Press**

Abbey Press
features Scripture quotes used by permission
from the New Revised Standard Version Bible,
copyrighted 1989.

Cover and book design by Mary E. Bolin.

ISBN 978-0-87029-653-6
Library of Congress 2014901710

Published by Abbey Press
1 Hill Drive • St. Meinrad, IN 47577
Printed by Abbey Press in the United States of America.

www.pathoflifebooks.com

Contents

Chapter 1

"God, I'm Stressed Out!"

By Tom McGrath

I awoke one morning years ago in a panic, believing I no longer had the strength to carry on. It was a difficult time at work as disagreements with co-workers flared up and major deadlines loomed. I had hurt my back, and for months it had been a constant source of pain throughout the day and kept me from sleeping at night. In that state, I felt abandoned by God and at the end of my rope.

Then, my daughter, an artist, handed me a shoebox and said, "This is for you, Dad." Inside was a statue she'd made of Jesus, seated, looking kind and compassionate. In the box were also a dozen small stones.

"What are the stones for?" I asked.

"They represent your troubles and your worries," she said. "Whenever something is bothering you and you can't get free of it, just place your worry in Jesus' lap."

In the midst of my agitation, my daughter had shown me the way: when worries intrude, turn to Jesus.

Working your way through

Life today is full of stress, because life today is full of change. Sometimes stress is activated by events outside of us—people, situations, and things that seem to threaten our well-being. And often it comes from within—from the way we perceive and react to what's going on in our lives. So, are there healthy ways to respond to and recover from stress?

Jesus tells us, "I am the way" (John 14:6). And when it comes to dealing with stress, I have found that Jesus both *shows* the way and *is* the way to serenity. Jesus offers us the awesome gift of peace—not based on

---

Let nothing disturb thee; let nothing dismay thee;
All things pass; God never changes.
Patience attains all that it strives for.
He who has God finds he lacks nothing.
God alone suffices.

—St. Teresa of Avila

always-changing exterior outcomes, but grounded in a relationship with the Father, who is always present and forever faithful. Let's look to Jesus for wise ways that counter stress and guide our feet on the path to peace.

✠ *Jesus understood fear.* Jesus understood the entangled relationship between fear and faith. His advice to avoid fear appears more than 100 times in the Gospels. Jesus also understood that faith can ease our fears and bring them down to size. Will we live controlled by fear? Or will we live our lives walking in faith?

By being faithful even in the face of suffering and death, Jesus showed how faith overcomes fear and leads us to eternal life. And we enter into this eternal life the moment we first believe. Deepening our trust and reliance on God leads us to a level of peace that prevents our worries from getting the better of us.

Here are a few practical ways to nurture faith when tempted to fear:

- Practice courage. Fortitude is a gift of the Holy Spirit.

- Borrow from the courage and faith of others. Look to the example of the saints, Jesus, and the good people in your life today.

• Be strengthened by Jesus in the Eucharist. He offers himself as food for the journey.

• If stress is causing you to doubt, pray "Lord, I believe; help my unbelief"(Mark 9:24).

✠ *Jesus always remembered who he was.* After so many urgings to avoid fear at all costs, Jesus surprises his disciples, saying "I will warn you whom to fear: fear him who, after he has killed, has authority to cast into hell [Gehenna in many translations]. Yes, I tell you, fear him" (Luke 12:5). Gehenna had been a place where human sacrifices were made to appease the pagan god Moloch. Jesus says to fear the one who tells you, "You are worth nothing, garbage to be cast aside." Then Jesus assures us that we are precious in the eyes of God. "Even the hairs of your head are all counted," he says two verses later.

As a spiritual director, I've come to see how often people cling to belief systems that convince them that if they make one false move, the bottom will fall out and the greatest fear beneath every other great fear will come true—they will be revealed as worthless, useless, a nobody. And so they add to their stress by upping the stakes—believing that their very dignity, worth, and existence as a person is on the line. At that point I want to shake them and say, "Do you know who you really are?"

> "Come to me, all you that are weary
> and are carrying heavy burdens,
> and I will give you rest."
>
> —Matthew 11:28

At his Baptism, Jesus heard his true identity revealed, "You are my Son, the Beloved; with you I am well pleased" (Mark 1:11). We all need to hear that message personally and take it to heart: "You are my beloved daughter. You are my beloved son." Saint Paul attests to this, "You have received a spirit of adoption. When we cry, 'Abba! Father!' it is that very Spirit bearing witness with our spirit that we are children of God" (Romans 8:15-16). At every challenge, Jesus handled the stress in his life by clinging to the truth of his divine identity. We can, too.

In times of stress:

• Recall that you are a child of God, created for a reason and a purpose.

• Know that as an heir of God, you have the right to ask God for aid and comfort in every situation you face.

• Seek first the reign of God in your life; a way will open up for you.

✠ *Jesus prayed.* "Come away to a deserted place all by yourselves and rest a while," Jesus told his apostles (Mark 6:31), and by extension, us. Jesus led a life of prayer and taught his disciples to pray. He revealed that he and the Father are one, and invited us into that blessed communion through prayer as well. Our task is to let the life of God flow into us and through us so we might bear great fruit.

So, when you are feeling stressed out, examine your prayer practices and patterns. Oftentimes when I'm stressed, my good habits of prayer go out the window. I let them lapse because "I haven't got time." This is exactly when I *should* be increasing my prayer rather than abandoning it. As St. Francis de Sales said, "Pray every day for a half hour, unless you are busy; then pray for an hour."

In his book *Praying the Truth*, William Barry, S.J., says we should pray not only "about" our stress, but from the depths of our stress. Tell God the truth about your life circumstances. Barry says God wants our friendship and tells us, "Let me reveal myself to you [as] you reveal yourself to me."

Don't hide your anxieties from God. Pray from your truth, and divine help will no longer be distant because you have invited God to get close.

- Take regular breaks from stress by creating a sacred space and time in your day in which you can rest in God.

- Meditate on Jesus' invitation: "Come to me, all you that are weary and are carrying heavy burdens, and I will give you rest" (Matthew 11:28).

- Once you have become calm, feel yourself immersed in the presence of God. Rest there.

✠ *Jesus knew human emotions.* Jesus is both fully God and fully man. Therefore, we can turn to Jesus knowing that he understands anything that we are going through. When Jesus was told that his friend Lazarus had died, he wept (John 11:35). On the night before he died, he experienced intense anguish. He told his apostles Peter, James, and John, "I am deeply grieved, even to death. Remain here, and keep awake" (Mark 14:34). And yet they fell asleep.

Sometimes when we experience great stress and the emotions that arise from our pain, we can choose unhealthy ways to cope. Like the apostles, we can simply zone out and not stay "awake"—through procrastination, avoidance, or the numerous ways life offers us to dull our senses. People use media, videogames, shopping, eating, drinking, obsessive relationships, and many other things to try to quiet the fear. But these methods work only in the short term, and in time only make things worse— sometimes *much* worse.

Jesus neither tried to run from stressful situations with their accompanying painful emotions nor did he let them shake his faith—in the Father, in himself, or in the work he was sent to do.

Choose healthy ways to rest and recuperate from stress such as:

• Exercise.

Peace I leave with you;
my peace I give to you.
I do not give to you as the world gives.
Do not let your hearts be troubled,
and do not let them be afraid.

—John 14:27

• Meditation.

• Relaxing with friends who help you be at your best.

Take heart

Our lives may be full of stress, but we can look to the life and teaching of Jesus to discover ways to moderate the forces in life that turn stress from a motivator into an enemy. Jesus shows us to:

• Not be fooled by fear.

• Recall our true identity as a beloved son or daughter of God.

• Weave habits of prayer into our days.

• Practice healthy ways to handle stress, resting in God who offers us a peace the world cannot give.

Through these simple means, we turn to Jesus, who calls out to us: "Do not be afraid, little flock, for it is your Father's good pleasure to give you the kingdom" (Luke 12:32).

Tom McGrath *is vice president of new product development at Loyola Press. He is the author of* Raising Faith-Filled Kids *(Loyola Press) and* Stress Therapy *(Abbey Press). He and his wife Kathleen live in Chicago.*

Chapter 11

How Sunday Offers God's Rest to the Weary

By Fr. Kurt Stasiak, O.S.B.

"Tomorrow is Sunday. We have to go to Church." Hearing Mom and Dad's weekly reminder was part of growing up Catholic. "Remember to keep holy the Lord's Day" may be the third of the Ten Commandments God handed over to Moses on Mount Sinai, but it was the first commandment I learned as a child.

Do you remember how Sundays used to be? I remember when Sunday really was a day of rest, a day when most things did seem to "shut down." Driving home from Sunday Mass, my parents and I would pass store after store, each one of them dark and empty.

Yes, there would be the occasional 24/7 gas station or the mini-grocery/pharmacy, but my parents explained these were for "emergency use only," and that non-essential items such as cigarettes and alcohol would certainly not be sold today! After all, Sunday was not a day to indulge. It was a special day—a day to go to church, and a day of rest.

Working your way through

Ask someone today what Sunday is like, and you're likely to hear, "sleeping till noon, not having to shave or get dressed up, having a real late brunch—and maybe even managing an afternoon nap." And for many

---

Just as God rested on the seventh day
from all his work which he had done (Genesis 2:2),
human life has a rhythm of work and rest.
The institution of the Lord's Day
helps everyone enjoy adequate rest
and leisure to cultivate their
familial, cultural, social, and religious lives.

—*Catechism of the Catholic Church*, No. 2184

people, Sunday is not even that kind of a day of rest. Instead it's the day to tackle the week's leftover tasks and chores, or fit in other activities. The idea of the leisurely "Sunday drive" through the countryside has yielded to the somewhat over-the-speed-limit race to the grocery store, the hardware store, the "Miscellaneous-R-Us," to youth sporting events, and what have you.

I can still hear my parents, though. "Tomorrow is Sunday. We have to go to church." *But why? What's so special about Sunday, anyway?*

✠ *You who worship God, stand still!* Sabbath comes from the Hebrew word *shabbat*, meaning "to cease, to desist." The Sabbath, which our Christian tradition has come to celebrate on Sunday, is a day to depart from the routines of the week, a day to put a momentary hold on earning our living "by the sweat of our brow." The Sabbath, Sunday, is a day for rest.

But let's be clear about what we mean by "rest." To consider Sunday a day of rest is not to dedicate a day to laziness or inactivity. So when we are encouraged to follow the example of "God rest[ing] on the seventh day from all the work that he had done" (Genesis 2:2), what does this mean? When we think of God "resting on the seventh day," what exactly comes to mind?

God's Sabbath "rest" was not some solemn slumber brought on because God had worn himself out earlier in the week! God "uses" the Sabbath to enjoy his work, not to recover from it! "[God's rest is] a contemplative gaze which does not look to new accomplishments but enjoys the beauty of what has already been achieved" (*The Day of the Lord*, paragraph 11). God's rest on the seventh day is for us both a model and a challenge. The Sabbath rest is not a time of emptiness. Rather, it is "something sacred because it is [our] way of withdrawing from the sometime excessively demanding cycle of earthly tasks in order to renew [our] awareness that everything is the work of God" (*The Day of the Lord*, 65).

We believe God is always present to us. Unfortunately, we are not always very present to God. The injunction to "remember the Sabbath day, and keep it holy" can be thought of as an obligation. But it can also be considered God's service to us—*a gift*. This "Day of the Lord" offers us the opportunity—the time—to present ourselves to God and return to him. Sunday encourages us to pay special attention to the God who is always with us, much like a wedding anniversary "interrupts" the ordinary calendar of husband and wife by giving them the reason and the opportunity to recall that they belong to each other. As Pope John Paul II remarked,

"God blessed the seventh day and hallowed it,
because on it God rested from all the work
that he had done in creation."

—Genesis 2:3

Through Sunday rest, daily concerns and tasks can find their proper perspective: the material things about which we worry give way to spiritual values; in a moment of encounter and less pressured exchange, we see the true face of the people with whom we live. Even the beauties of nature—too often marred by the desire to exploit, which turns against man himself—can be rediscovered and enjoyed to the full (*The Day of the Lord*, 67).

Guests to our monastery often ask, "How do you monks get anything done? It seems like every time you get going, you stop and go to church and pray!" Well, it's not quite like that. But in the monastery, our prayer *does* regularly interrupt our work. However, we don't consider that inefficiency. We consider it an act of thanksgiving for the day we have been given, and an opportunity to thank the Giver of the day. We need reminders—opportunities—like that, because all of us, even in the monastery, can get so lost in what we are doing that we lose our sense of the One behind it all.

✠ *Sunday Eucharist.* The Church considers the
Sunday Eucharist "the foundation and confirmation of
all Christian practice" (*Catechism of the Catholic Church*,
No. 2181), and so obliges us to participate each week,
unless a serious reason intervenes. (A serious reason
would include caring for a sick family member or friend,
our own illness or infirmity, or a dispensation given by
our pastor.)

Most likely, Mass is celebrated in your parish every
day. But why, on this *one* day, do we have this obligation to
attend and participate? Simply put, the Sunday obligation
assures us that on this Day of the Lord we should not be
merely "left to ourselves." Instead, on this day we make
a special effort to hand ourselves over to the Lord.

When your parish comes together for Sunday Mass,
the gathering offers more than safety in numbers. As
important as our private prayer is, we experience a unique
treasure in our community prayer. The fifth-century
bishop (and saint) John Chrysostom explained it to his
people this way:

> You cannot pray at home as at church, where there is a
> great multitude, where exclamations are cried out to God
> as from one great heart, and where there is something
> more: the union of minds, the accord of souls, the bond
> of charity, the prayers of the priests (Cited in *Catechism*,
> No. 2179).

So important was this to the early Christians that long before Sunday became a publicly observed day of rest, they would rise before dawn to come together and keep holy the Lord's day. Rising while it's still dark may not be our idea of taking a rest, but their practice shouts out the importance this day had for them. The Day of the Lord was important because the Lord was important!

✠ *"Remember to keep holy the Lord's day."* How can we approach Sunday not merely as a day of obligation, but as a day of recreation—a "re-creation" of our heart, mind, and soul? Here are several suggestions:

1. Prepare for the Sunday Eucharist. Spending even a few minutes Saturday evening or Sunday morning looking at the Scripture readings is an easy way to open ourselves to God's words to us. And, setting aside our usual busyness may mean taking the time to arrive at church early (we do this for important meetings or events, don't we?), so we can settle in and set our hearts and minds at rest.

2. Sunday offers us the opportunity to interrupt the work we do for "survival" and provide a charitable work on behalf of others. As the *Catechism* states, "Sunday is traditionally consecrated by Christian piety to good works and humble service of the sick, the infirm, and the elderly" (No. 2186). Giving to others is one way of giving thanks for what God has given us.

3. A meal at a restaurant may be one way of enjoying a Sunday rest with family and friends, but that same place and time means work for those who prepare and serve your meals. No matter which side of the table you're on—whether you are the diner or the server—you can still help make the day holy by making an extra effort to be charitable, helpful, and respectful to those around you.

4. There are many for whom Sunday is seldom a day of rest. Police officers, firefighters, medical personnel, and essential service personnel—these people deserve a special place in our prayers. And in some small way, our reliance upon their availability and readiness may remind us of God's constant care.

5. Finally, a reminder that observing a day of rest does not mean hiding ourselves from the world. Indeed,

---

"It is necessary to promote reflection and efforts at reconciling
the demands of work with those of the family
and to recover the true meaning of the feast,
especially on Sunday,
the weekly Easter, the Day of the Lord and the day of man,
the day of the family, of the community, and of solidarity."

—Pope Benedict XVI

"Christians will also sanctify Sunday by devoting time and care to their families and relatives, [something] often difficult to do on other days of the week" (*Catechism*, No. 2186). Sunday can be a day to re-establish, maintain, and strengthen relationships. Like that wedding anniversary, it can be a day to simply be with someone who needs—and treasures—our presence.

✠ ***Sunday, the day of re-creation.*** Jesus did not invent Sunday as a day of the week, but his rising from the dead certainly puts the meaning of this day "in a whole new light." From Easter Sunday on, even the rising sun pays tribute to the Risen Son of God! As the *Catechism* remarks, Sunday "symbolizes the new creation ushered in by God's Resurrection" (No. 2174).

Sunday is a day to celebrate the new life granted to us by the resurrected Christ, and to share that joy with one another. Setting aside a special day to step back, slow down, and recall the grace of this truth is necessary to understanding how God is at work in our lives. Additionally, the spiritual rest we are afforded on Sunday strengthens our wearied souls to participate more fully in God's re-creation of the world the rest of the week through the Body of Christ of which we are each a part.

Take heart

Remember. That's the first word of the Sunday precept in the Book of Exodus. "Remember to keep holy the Lord's Day." Sunday is *the* day to remember—to remember God's gifts, to remember the blessings we enjoy, to remember what God asks of us.

Sunday is not a special day because we are obliged to be in church. We are obliged to be in church because it is a special day. As the psalmist says, "This is the day the Lord has made. Let us be glad and rejoice in it" (Psalm 118:24).

Fr. Kurt Stasiak, O.S.B., a monk of Saint Meinrad Archabbey, serves as the monastery's prior. He also teaches sacramental theology and serves as a spiritual director in Saint Meinrad Seminary and School of Theology. He is the author of four books on the sacraments, including A Confessor's Handbook, *revised and expanded edition (Paulist, 2010).*

Chapter III

Finding Strength of Spirit in the Midst of a Busy Life

By Gerilyn H. Leibfarth

Along with my duties as director of religious education in my parish, I serve as the middle school liturgist. As part of this job, I set up for Mass every Thursday morning. I get the sacred gifts and altar vessels ready, along with the music and sound systems. I put out the necessary books. I even turn on the lights and microphone!

I can be quite the "Martha." Yet, I am also quite the "Mary." Let me explain.

For the longest time, I understood the focus of the biblical story of Jesus visiting the home of Martha and Mary (Luke 10:38-42) to be on letting go of our busyness, slowing down, and spending time with Jesus, "the better part." Now I see this passage as a call to conversion. It was not *what* Martha was doing that was the issue, but *why* she was doing it. Often in the Gospels we hear Jesus criticize the Pharisees who followed the letter of the law while ignoring its spirit. This was Martha's problem. Being a good Jewish woman, she chose to deal with the "details of hospitality" and "household tasks," seeing these as mere duties to be completed. Jesus' challenge to Martha—and to you and me—is a change in attitude, from grudging duty to loving service.

Like us, Martha was being called to conversion, a personal relationship with God through Jesus. When we

---

We must pray without ceasing,
in every occurrence and employment of our lives—
that prayer which is rather a habit
of lifting up the heart to God
as in a constant communication with him.

—St. Elizabeth Ann Seton

embrace God's love, this love cannot be contained, but needs to flow through *everything* we do. We enter into this graced relationship at Baptism. We take on Christ. His mission of love becomes our mission.

Working your way through

I can empathize with Martha. I am what many refer to as a "cradle Catholic." I was born to parents who are Catholic, was baptized, raised, and educated in the faith. I was blessed with a firm foundation in my faith. Yet my personal relationship with Christ was like that of Martha. I did everything I was *supposed* to do: attended Mass every Sunday, took part in the Sacrament of Reconciliation, and performed all the "duties" expected of good Catholics. I had great "head" knowledge of Christ; however, I did not have an *affective* knowledge. All head, no heart.

A retreat during my freshman year in college altered my perspective. The experience held the key to my conversion, and life has not been the same since. The *National Directory of Catechesis* states that "the Christian Faith is, above all, conversion to Jesus Christ. It is the fruit of God's grace and the free response to the prompting of the Holy Spirit. It arises from the depths of the human person and involves such a profound transformation of heart and mind that it causes the believer to change radically both internally and externally." God fills us with sanctifying grace at Baptism. He sends his Holy Spirit to guide us in using this grace in transforming our lives. He gave us his Son to light the path. As beloved children of God, we have only to open and surrender our hearts and wills to him.

This is the "better part" that Mary understood and practiced at the feet of Jesus. This posture—letting go of pride and living in God's love—is what real conversion is: a lifelong process of responding to God's call. And for us "busy Catholics," this process is sustained and strengthened by prayer and in the Eucharist. I hope to reflect with you on how this occurs so that you may find strength of spirit in the midst of your busy life.

✠ *Responding to God.* In her book *Full of Grace,* Johnnette Benkovic states, "All prayer is simply a response to God's unconditional love for us and his invitation to experience that love. In prayer, God lifts our hearts and minds to him as we desire to completely surrender to his action in us. Through prayer, God calls us into intimacy with him, an intimacy that transforms us, an intimacy that imbues us with his presence, an intimacy that is life-giving."

Directly following the account of Martha and Mary in Luke's Gospel is a passage in which Jesus teaches his

> "You are worried and distracted by many things;
> there is need of only one thing."
>
> —Luke 10:41-42

---

disciples to pray, and then offers words of encouragement to persevere in prayer. Jesus was a person of prayer. He is the perfect pray-er. What is prayer but a dialogue with God? Jesus is the Word of love spoken to us by the heavenly Father, and he is our response.

In the midst of our busy lives, prayer is a transformative fountain of grace. "The good person out of the good treasure of the heart produces good, and the evil person out of evil treasure produces evil," Jesus says in Luke 6:45. "It is out of the abundance of the heart that the mouth speaks." Consider how our everyday relationships reflect our own image and influence who we are. Prayer calls us to be in relationship with the One who is Love. It calls us to imitate and live in that love. Prayer connects us with the "good treasure," the "better part" which helps us keep our focus each and every day.

✠ ***Pray without ceasing.*** Again, Benkovic states, "we should be faithful to a time of prayer no matter when it occurs in the course of the day." Imagine making a list of the work you have accomplished today and a list of the times you prayed. Would you be discouraged to find that your chore list is longer? The challenge is to make this a *single* list. Like Martha, we have this idea that we must accomplish all our tasks *before* we can pray.

I propose that we *can* do what Martha is doing, while at the same time inwardly sitting at the feet of Jesus and listening to him as Mary did. We must, as St. Paul says, "pray without ceasing" (1 Thessalonians 5:17).

God is to be found in the midst of our experiences, in the *now*. To pray without ceasing is to have all we do and say reflect the love God has for us. The attitude of Christ needs to impregnate our words and deeds. *Our very person must be a prayer.* True conversion of heart means that we submit all our thoughts, words, and actions to the guidance of the Holy Spirit, which "helps us in our weakness; for we do not know how to pray as we ought, but that very Spirit intercedes with sighs too deep for words" (Romans 8:26).

✠ *Eucharist as ultimate encounter.* The Eucharist is the ultimate conversion experience, the ultimate encounter with Christ. Consider Martha's transformation. When she is introduced to us in Luke's Gospel, she is busied about, "worried and distracted by many things." She is not focused, like her sister Mary, on Jesus, the one thing necessary. Later, however, in John's Gospel, in the wake of her brother Lazarus' death, she proclaims, "Yes, Lord, I believe that you are the Messiah, the Son of God, the one coming into the world" (11:27). Here, her focus is properly centered. Her encounter with Christ turned her whole life around.

The Eucharist, as "source and summit of Christian life" (*Lumen Gentium*, 11), is meant to do the same in our lives. Essentially, the Eucharist is about relationship. Jesus in the Eucharist longs to be one with us; he nourishes us, and unites us with himself.

Regularly celebrating and receiving the Eucharist with faith is important because our vocation is to lead *others* to know and love Christ. The Body and Blood of Christ, our spiritual food, gradually transforms us into the image of Christ. Part of this transformation is a more selfless love for God and for others.

The Eucharist affects how we live. If we live in love, then—as St. Augustine wrote—we become what we receive. We become Eucharist for others by giving of ourselves in our daily lives, in every thought, in every good act we do, in every form of outreach to our sisters and brothers. Our relationship with Christ leads us down paths perhaps we cannot foresee; asking us to give up things that we cling to so there is more room for God and others. In this way, we are equipped to keep our focus on Christ, as did John's Martha.

Take heart

Author and lecturer Leo Buscaglia once talked about a contest he was asked to judge. The purpose of the contest was to find the most caring child. The winner was a 4-year-old boy whose next-door neighbor was an elderly gentleman who had recently lost his wife. Upon seeing the man cry, the little boy went into the man's yard, climbed into his lap, and just sat there. When his mother asked what he had said to the neighbor, the little boy said, "Nothing; I just helped him cry."

This little one demonstrates how we must become what we receive in Christ. Strengthened by prayer and

---

Pray every day for a half hour,
unless you are busy; then, pray for an hour.

—St. Francis de Sales

the Eucharist, we must carry on Christ's mission of love in building up the Kingdom of God. And you can do this right *now*, in the midst of your ordinary, daily activities and encounters. Like Mary, first choose the "better part," and then like Martha, put your abilities at the service of others—not grudgingly, but out of love.

***Gerilyn H. Leibfarth** has served as the Director of Religious Education since 1993 at St. Michael the Archangel Parish, Findlay, Ohio. She has a Bachelor of Arts in Religious Studies from the College of Mount St. Joseph in Cincinnati and a Master of Arts in Theological Studies from the University of Dayton.*

Chapter IV

How the Saints Help Us Through Hardship

By Silas Henderson

Sickness and physical disability, emotional and psychological illness, and death are all parts of the human experience. Yet, even while we are in the midst of such trials, God's grace remains with us. As St. Paul says, "I am convinced that neither death, nor life, nor angels, nor rulers, nor things present, nor things to come, nor powers, nor height, nor depth, nor anything else in creation, will be able to separate us from the love of God in Christ Jesus our Lord" (Romans 8:38-39).

Still, while our *heads* may reassure us of God's presence through our darkest moments, our *hearts* are often overwhelmed by fear, anxiety, and sadness, among other things. These very real feelings can challenge our faith and ability to hope. Sometimes these feelings can be so consuming that we can give up hoping at all, doubting even God's presence and love.

Working your way through

Some years ago, I met Mary, a patient in a large urban hospital where I was working as a chaplain. Mary had been in the hospital for several weeks and was facing a broad assortment of painful and complicated health issues. Before her illness, Mary had been very active in her parish and had even been involved in her parish's ministry to the sick and shut-ins. Without a family of her own, her parish had become her family.

They contemplate God, praise him, and constantly care
for those whom they have left on earth. . . .
Their intercession is their most exalted service to God's plan.
We can and should ask them to intercede for us
and for the whole world.

—*Catechism of the Catholic Church*, No. 2683

Now, after a long time in the hospital, she was sinking into despair. Her anguish was not brought on by the severity of her illness, but rather because she believed she had been forgotten by her church and by God. On my first day with Mary, I listened as she tried to put her feelings of sadness and isolation into words.

As time passed, I and other chaplains and hospital staff members became Mary's community. Our visits gave her something to look forward to. We were recognizing that she was there, and we were investing in her, sharing her burden with her. This was a powerful reminder for me that we are all called to bear one another's burdens and bring God's grace and peace to one another.

✠ *The communion of saints.* In our Christian tradition, this is beautifully expressed in the communion of saints, the community of believers, past and present, united in Christ. This belief makes us aware that we are not only responsible for one another, but we are one with each other. No one is alone. Our God-given vocation is to help one another to face the present and future with hope, to be strong for one another, even to carry each other.

In learning how to carry our crosses, we not only have the support of those who are here with us now. We also have the witness and prayers of those holy men and women who have gone before us. The saints can help us to recognize the presence of God in our own trials and suffering because—just like us—they faced sickness, physical disability, emotional and psychological illness, loss, loneliness, anxiety, fear, exhaustion, and death. They were able to recognize the graces hidden in human suffering.

By learning their stories and getting to know them as the people they were and are, we recognize that they have much to say. I offer below some short reflections about four specific individuals who may serve as role models and inspirations in times of hardship.

✠ *Blessed Margaret of Castello: Companion in physical disability and abandonment.* Margaret was born to a noble Italian family in 1287. Blind, lame, and physically deformed, she suffered from her parents' neglect. Her parents denied that they even had a daughter, and refused to give her a name.

After Margaret's identity was discovered, her parents took her to a local shrine to pray for a cure, but when their prayer was not answered, they abandoned her. After living for some time as a beggar, she was accepted as a member of the Third Order of Saint Dominic, in whose home she lived the rest of her short life. Margaret died in 1320 at the age of 33.

In spite of her abandonment and rejection, Margaret was able to go beyond her physical limitations, seeing God's love for her in the community that surrounded her and in those for whom she cared. She let herself fall in love with God, and understood that no amount of human rejection or physical challenge could separate her from that love.

✠ *Saint Aloysius Gonzaga: Companion in terminal illness.* Aloysius, who was born in 1568, was a prince of the Holy Roman Empire. At an early age he felt a call to give himself completely to God in a life of service as a

Jesuit priest. The prince begged his father for permission to renounce his titles and inheritance. After years of struggle and conflict, he received permission to leave behind his old life and begin a new life of poverty, chastity, and obedience.

He traveled to Rome at age 17 to become a Jesuit. Although he had been a strong and healthy child, a series of illnesses and extreme penitential practices took a toll on his body. Because of his weak physical health, his superiors were reluctant to allow Aloysius to serve in the hospitals when a plague broke out in Rome in 1591. He obediently accepted their orders and served when and where he was allowed.

Early that same year, however, Aloysius found a man lying in the street. Without regard for his own safety, he picked up the man and carried him to the hospital. It was in this way that he contracted the disease from which his superiors hoped to protect him. Despite his strong spirit and mind, Aloysius suffered for more than four months before he died on June 21, 1591. He was 24 years old.

During his final months, he used what little strength he had to visit and pray for those in the hospital with him. He offered his sufferings to God as a prayer for those who had no one to pray for them. In our own sufferings and fears about what the future might hold, Aloysius offers us a model for seeing beyond the limits of our afflictions and trusting that God always remains with us.

✠ ***Blessed Basil Hopko: Companion in depression and despair.*** Basil was born in the Austro-Hungarian Empire in 1904. Ordained to the priesthood in Prague, he dedicated himself to ministry in parishes and to training young men for the priesthood. He was made a bishop in 1947. Following the Communist takeover of the former Czechoslovakia, this holy bishop was arrested in 1950. He was repeatedly tortured and denied food and water before being sentenced to prison, where he remained until 1964.

During his imprisonment, Basil began to suffer from depression and despair. At the end of his life he remembered: "I became only a shadow of a human being, hardly able to walk. I lost even the desire to live." Despite his severe depression, Basil never lost hope. Although he struggled to pray and to recognize God's presence in the midst of his sufferings and abuse, he also knew that it was God's loving presence that ultimately saved him from his inner darkness.

Transferred to a home for the elderly, he was a broken man who never recovered his physical or emotional health. Basil Hopko died in 1976.

In our own struggles with sadness, despair, or depression, Basil Hopko serves as a guide for us, reminding us that God's love and support are always there for us, carrying us, holding us, even in our darkest moments.

✠ *Venerable Matt Talbot: Companion in facing addiction.* Matt was born to a poor Irish family in 1856. He began drinking when he was 12 and soon became a chronic alcoholic. An unskilled laborer, he spent most of his wages on alcohol, and he was soon deep in debt.

In 1884, finally worn down and frustrated by his dependence on alcohol, Matt decided to "take the pledge" (renouncing alcohol) for a period of three months, then six months, and then for life. He successfully remained

---

Every Mass invites us, the saints on earth, to sing
"Holy, holy, holy Lord,"
in company with all the angels and saints.
In Jesus, crucified and risen,
the boundary between the living
and the dead has been erased.

—Carol Luebering

sober for the next 40 years but he was not alone in his struggle. He had the support of a number of close friends, and he found comfort and strength in his faith.

He became devoted to prayer, attended Mass daily, and supported a number of charities. Known for his generosity to the poor, his spirit of prayer, and his simple life, he was loved by those who knew him. Matt Talbot died June 7, 1925, as he walked to morning Mass.

Although Matt was able to remain sober for 40 years, sobriety was a struggle. He once told his sister, "Never look down on a man who cannot give up the drink. It is easier to get out of hell." Matt Talbot offers us his own life as a lesson for facing addiction. Self-discipline, prayer, support, and trust in God were his weapons in fighting his lifelong battle with addiction. In our battles, he stands before us as someone who understands the pain and power of addiction, extending his hand, and offering to be our companion in times of darkness and doubt.

Take heart

The Letter to the Hebrews reminds us that we are surrounded by a "great cloud of witnesses" (12:1) who support us, teach us, pray for us and with us. Our membership in the communion of saints reminds us that even in the darkness of sickness, suffering, anxiety, weariness, and death, we are never alone. God has sent his saints— those who have gone before us and those who are with us now—to watch over us, to be with us, and to help us find the courage, hope, and faith to trust in God's promise of eternal life.

Silas Henderson *serves on the staff of Abbey Press and has written numerous articles on prayer and spirituality. He is the editor of* Deacon Digest *magazine and author of* From Season to Season: A Book of Saintly Wisdom.

Chapter V

How the Eucharist Makes Whole the Broken

By Fr. Matthias Neuman, O.S.B.

The funeral Mass produced a great outpouring of grief. The young man was in his mid-20s and a student for the priesthood when he succumbed to a rare blood disease. The youngest of seven children, he was deeply mourned and missed by his parents and his older brothers and sisters. They wept softly and comforted each other during Mass. Later his mother said, "We miss him so much, but it was such a comfort to pray for him and, we believe, with him at Mass."

Another woman and her family rejoiced at the news of her pregnancy, particularly when she received the

Eucharist at Mass because "this little life had already begun to know the joy of the Lord through me!" Eight months later the family grieved as that small life was extinguished in the womb, but they remain grateful for the meaning of that life, and hopeful of the life to come: "Today we trust that she is in the presence of God, singing his praises with the choirs of angels. We join her in singing, here on earth, praising God at Mass, until we have the chance to join her in the heavenly choir!"

The Eucharist became a real life support for these families, blessing them in their brokenness and uniting them in the person of that nourishment—Jesus Christ.

Working your way through

"I am the bread of life," Jesus tells his followers after the multiplication of loaves in the Gospel of John. "I am the living bread that came down from heaven. Whoever eats of this bread will live forever; and the bread that I will give for the life of the world is my flesh" (John 6:35, 51).

After his death and resurrection, Jesus appeared to a few of his disciples who initially failed to recognize him until he made the Last Supper present to them again: "When he was at the table with them, he took bread, blessed and broke it, and gave it to them. Then

their eyes were opened, and they recognized him . . ."
(Luke 24:30-31).

As Christ's disciples today, we relive these events
even more fully and are transformed by them as we faith-
fully celebrate the Eucharist. The Scripture passages above
helped shape the tradition of the Church that gives us
the Eucharist—Christ himself, to nourish our souls for
eternal life. His real presence in the sacrament blesses us,
his sacrifice takes on our brokenness, and our communion
with him places us on the path to wholeness and holiness.

The Eucharist, Pope John Paul II said, reminds us of
the Paschal Mystery of Jesus; it offers praise and thanksgiving to God; it is the presence of Jesus Christ among
us; it is the bonding of a spiritual community with God;
it is the sacrifice of ourselves to God; it is the sacrifice
of Jesus Christ made present to us, and much more.

✠ *A sacrament of daily forgiveness and healing.*
The Eucharist is a sacrament of forgiveness and healing,
and of blessing and hope. "No other sacrament has
greater healing power. Through it sins are purged away,
virtues are increased, and the soul is enriched with an
abundance of every spiritual gift," said St. Thomas
Aquinas. "Eucharistic nourishment, instead of being
transformed into the one who takes it, transforms that
person into itself."

Forgiveness plays an integral role in the healing that so many people need. People need physical, psychological, and spiritual healing. Researchers are finding that the three kinds of healing are often woven together. The greatest healing we need is spiritual—to know and feel that we are in a right relationship with God. To truly know forgiveness enables growth in so many areas of life, and that is healing in itself.

The Eucharist can begin this process of spiritual healing. Several of the early Church Fathers—such as St. Ignatius of Antioch—liked to refer to the Eucharist as "divine medicine" or the "medicine of immortality."

Full, conscious, and active participation in the celebration of the Eucharist is one of the best medicines for the human heart that is anxious, weary, or hurting. It is

---

The Eucharist is "the food of the soul that maintains, mends, increases, and gladdens the life of grace in the soul, because it gives to it the very author of grace. The divine life can enter into us by other doors, but it is by Holy Communion that it inundates our souls like a river in a flood."

—Blessed Columba Marmion

a way to seek forgiveness for our lesser, habitual faults. These are the failings that occur in daily interactions with family members, friends, and co-workers. They may include anger, a critical tongue, envy, overindulgence, and so on. Each of us has our own particular faults that, no matter how hard we try to be rid of them, stay with us for a lifetime. Celebrating the Eucharist with devotion is one of the best ways to regularly seek forgiveness for these habitual failings.

This practice is solidly affirmed by the *Catechism of the Catholic Church*: "Daily conversion and penance find their source and nourishment in the Eucharist, for in it is made present the sacrifice of Christ who has reconciled us with God. Through the Eucharist those who live from the life of Christ are fed and strengthened. 'It is a remedy to free us from our daily faults and to preserve us from mortal sins'" (No. 1436).

Various points in the Mass connect the Eucharist and forgiveness. Beginning with the penitential rite, the Eucharist is a time when family members can recall their own failures in relating to one another, seek God's forgiveness together in praying the Our Father, and be reconciled at the Sign of Peace. We can then really mean the words we pray immediately before receiving the Eucharist: "Lord, I am not worthy that you should enter under my roof, but only say the word and my soul shall be healed."

✠ *A sacrament of blessing and hope.* The Eucharist is also the vine that gives life to its branches, as Jesus tells us in the Gospel of John (15:5). We may think of the Eucharist as a spiritual food, as strength for the journey of life, as the promise of the future heavenly banquet. But how often do we think of the celebration of the Eucharist as Jesus saying "I love you" to each one of us personally?

This outpouring of love from vine to branches is what happens in each and every Eucharist. The great willingness of Jesus Christ to give himself as food and drink saves, nourishes, forgives, and heals all those who receive him in faith and love. At the same time, the Body and Blood of Christ imparts value, worth, and blessing.

This blessedness flows from the love that Jesus extends to us. Every act of love bestows value and worth on the beloved. Jesus' love, as an act of divine love, makes us blessed. To receive value and worth restores our wholeness and makes us well. In dealing especially with personal trials and hardships, the Eucharist helps us remember our blessedness in the sight of God.

"Jesus is the vine, we are the branches, grace is the sap which goes up into the branches so as to make them bear fruit," wrote Blessed Columba Marmion. "It is

---

above all, through the gift of himself in the Eucharist that Christ makes grace abound in us."

Physical contact with the person of Christ is what provides this grace that restores wholeness. In the Gospel accounts, those who touch Jesus with expectant faith, or who are touched by him, are healed of their various afflictions.

"[They] brought all who were sick to him, and begged him that they might touch even the fringe of his cloak; and all who touched it were healed," the Gospel of Matthew tells us (14:35-36). A woman afflicted with hemorrhages for 12 years did this very thing, the Gospel of Luke relates (8:43-48), and was immediately healed.

Jesus is truly, really, and substantially present in the Eucharist under the appearance of bread and wine, a mystery that requires us to "walk by faith, not by sight" (2 Corinthians 5:7). By his lasting presence in this sacrament, we are invited to touch him, be touched by him, and be healed. However, he is not to be approached casually or skeptically, but with the reverent, expectant faith of the hemorrhaging woman.

"The Eucharist is not merely some abstract, spiritual contact with Jesus. In the Eucharist we have direct physical contact with Jesus," says Fr. John Hampsch, C.M.F. "In the Eucharist, we touch Jesus and Jesus touches us."

✠ *A blessed future ahead.* The healing power of Jesus as recounted in the Gospels points to something far deeper and longer-lasting than *physical* wholeness. It is a sign of God's powerful love and desire to touch and heal our *souls*, reconcile us with one another, and restore us to union with him—in time and eternity. This love of Jesus, shown in each celebration of the

---

May your sacrament, O Jesus, be light to the mind,
strength to the will, joy to the heart.
May it be the support of the weak,
the comfort of the suffering,
the wayfaring bread of salvation for the dying,
and for all the "pledge of future glory." Amen.

—Pope John XXIII

Eucharist, makes us blessed and also gives us the promise of future glory.

This promise is made to us through the Resurrection of Christ. The Eucharist, which reminds us of the Paschal Mystery and makes it present for us, is the promise of our own future resurrection. This promise infinitely fulfills and exceeds those God made in the Old Testament in creating us and making us his own. We are reminded of the return of Jesus and God's pledge to "make all things new" through him (Revelation 21:5).

Each celebration of the Eucharist calls us to remember God's promise of resurrection, and at the same time, reassess our varied hopes in its light. All our intermediate hopes should be directed to that last, *great* hope. Even when much seems lost in our lives, the Eucharist powerfully reminds us that there is still a blessed future ahead.

Take heart

As forgiveness and healing, as blessing and hope, the Eucharist is support and comfort for those who are hurting, weary, or anxious. The Eucharist makes real the words of Jesus: "I am with you always, to the end of the age" (Matthew 28:20). He remains with us in many ways, but most fully in the Eucharist because it is *Christ himself.*

Let us find our strength in the presence of Jesus and put our trust in his promise: "I am the resurrection and the life" (John 11:25). Whatever might be the pains, fears, or losses in our lives, the Eucharist is our life support, nourishing us and transforming us for eternal life. "The food that you receive," said St. Ambrose, "that living bread which came down from heaven, supplies the very substance of eternal life, and whoever will eat it, will never die, for it is the body of Christ."

Fr. Matthias Neuman, O.S.B., is a monk of Saint Meinrad Archabbey. He was ordained in 1967 and received his Doctorate in Systematic Theology from San Anselmo Pontifical University in Rome in 1975. He is currently the chaplain for the Benedictine Sisters at Our Lady of Grace Monastery in Beech Grove, Indiana, and teaches theology classes at Saint Meinrad School of Theology's campus in Indianapolis.